LITTLE

AND

HIS TRACHEOSTOMY

SAVANNAH ABELS NUCCIO

ISBN: 9798870527543

Edited by Emma Lawson

Cover art and illustrations by Hasan Lai

Medical illustration by Shanta Das

Published by Amazon Kindle Direct Publishing in the USA.

To the Ruiz family, and to any family with a child who has a medical device or disability.

Our story begins with Little T,

the happiest turtle you would ever see.

He loves to run, play, and ride his bike.

But there's something about him that he does not like.

His mommy calls it his "special necklace,"

the tool that keeps him from going breathless.

His daddy says it gives him superpowers,

It helps him run, play, and ride his bike for hours.

"But Mommy and Daddy, you look different from me.

You don't have this necklace," says a worried Little T.

"We may look different, you can tell from the start,

but what really matters is what's inside your heart."

"But Mommy and Daddy, you can do things I can't.

What if the other kids won't give me a chance?"

"You are kind and funny and as sharp as a knife.

What would there be for them to not like?"

"But Mommy and Daddy, there is something I see.

You're always carrying a special bag of things for me."

"We bring this special bag along

so you'll stay healthy and strong."

"We love you for all that you are.

From your head to your toes, you shine like a star."

"I can do the things I love for hours.

Daddy, maybe this does give me superpowers."

"I can run, play, and ride my bike.

Mommy, maybe this necklace is something I like."

So our story ends with Little T,

the happiest turtle you would ever see...

who finally began to love his tracheostomy.

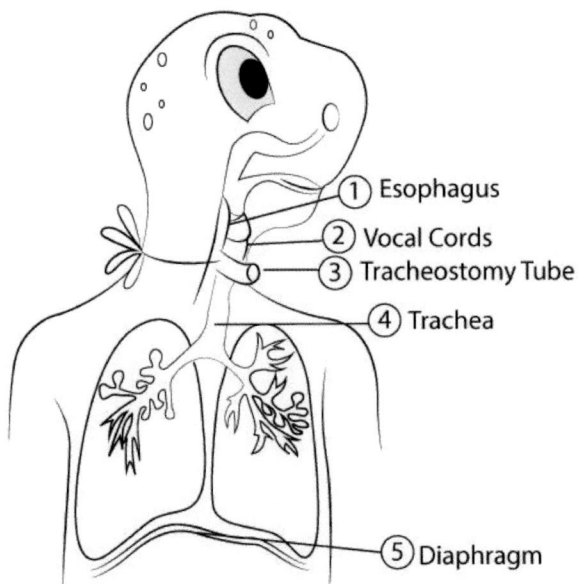

1. **Esophagus** – Like a slide at the playground, this helps move food and drinks from Little T's mouth to his throat and down into his tummy.

2. **Vocal Cords** – These help Little T talk, sing, and make sounds by vibrating against each other!

3. **Tracheostomy Tube** – This tube helps Little T get air into his lungs when he breathes in.

4. **Trachea** – This is like a really big straw that carries air from your nose and mouth into your lungs.

5. **Diaphragm** – Imagine jumping on a trampoline. When it moves down, air is pulled into Little T's lungs. When it moves up, air is pushed out!

Printed in Great Britain
by Amazon

58032416R00021